50 Mexican Recipes Beyond Tacos

By: Kelly Johnson

Table of Contents

- Enchiladas Verdes
- Chiles Rellenos
- Tamales
- Pozole
- Sopes
- Mole Poblano
- Quesadillas de Flor de Calabaza
- Guacamole with Roasted Garlic
- Chilaquiles
- Carne Asada Burritos
- Sopa de Lima
- Ceviche
- Baja Fish Tacos (with a twist)
- Mexican Street Corn (Elote)
- Fajitas
- Empanadas de Pollo
- Rajas con Crema

- Arroz con Pollo
- Pibil Tacos
- Tostadas de Tinga
- Mexi-Pasta Salad
- Prawn Aguachile
- Churros
- Chile con Carne
- Huevos Rancheros
- Mexican Rice
- Poblano Soup
- Capirotada (Mexican Bread Pudding)
- Mexican Cornbread
- Chorizo con Papas
- Molletes
- Panuchos
- Tacos de Carnitas
- Picadillo
- Salsa Verde
- Tarta de Tres Leches

- Caldo de Res
- Cochinita Pibil
- Birria
- Relleno de Pollo
- Papas con Chorizo
- Mexican Hot Chocolate
- Chilequiles Rojos
- Tacos de Lengua
- Pescado a la Veracruzana
- Salsa Roja
- Tostadas de Ceviche
- Tamal de Elote
- Tacos al Pastor
- Arroz con Leche

Enchiladas Verdes

Ingredients

- 12 corn tortillas
- 2 cups cooked chicken (shredded)
- 1 1/2 cups green salsa (salsa verde)
- 1/2 cup sour cream
- 1/2 cup shredded cheese (cheddar or Oaxaca)
- 1 small onion, chopped
- 1 tbsp olive oil
- 1 tbsp chopped cilantro (for garnish)
- Salt to taste

Instructions

1. Preheat your oven to 375°F (190°C).
2. Heat the tortillas in a skillet with a bit of oil until soft. Alternatively, you can heat them in the microwave for a few seconds.
3. Pour a thin layer of salsa verde in the bottom of a baking dish.
4. Dip each tortilla into the salsa, then fill with shredded chicken and a sprinkle of chopped onion. Roll the tortillas and place them seam-side down in the baking dish.
5. Top with the remaining salsa verde and sprinkle with shredded cheese.
6. Bake for 20 minutes, until the cheese is melted and bubbly.

7. Garnish with cilantro and serve with sour cream on the side.

Chiles Rellenos

Ingredients

- 6 poblano peppers
- 1 cup cheese (cheddar, Monterey Jack, or queso fresco)
- 1/2 lb ground beef or chicken (optional)
- 1 onion, chopped
- 2 tomatoes, chopped
- 2 eggs (separated into yolks and whites)
- 1/2 cup flour
- 1/4 cup vegetable oil
- Salt and pepper to taste

Instructions

1. Roast the poblano peppers over an open flame or under the broiler until the skin is charred. Place them in a plastic bag or covered bowl to steam, then peel off the skin.
2. Cut a slit down each pepper and remove the seeds.
3. Stuff each pepper with cheese, and optionally, cooked ground meat, onions, and chopped tomatoes.
4. In a bowl, beat the egg whites until stiff peaks form, then gently fold in the yolks.
5. Roll the stuffed peppers in flour, then dip them into the egg mixture.

6. Heat oil in a pan over medium heat and fry the peppers until golden brown on both sides.

7. Serve with tomato sauce or fresh salsa.

Tamales

Ingredients

- 2 cups masa harina
- 1 1/2 cups chicken broth
- 1/2 cup vegetable oil
- 1 tsp baking powder
- 1 tsp salt
- 2 cups cooked chicken or pork (shredded)
- 1/2 cup red or green salsa
- 24 corn husks (soaked in warm water for 30 minutes)

Instructions

1. In a bowl, combine masa harina, baking powder, salt, and vegetable oil. Gradually add chicken broth until the dough is soft and pliable.
2. To make the filling, combine the shredded chicken or pork with salsa.
3. Spread a small amount of masa dough onto the soaked corn husk, then add a spoonful of the filling. Fold the sides of the husk and roll it up tightly.
4. Arrange the tamales upright in a large steamer. Cover with a damp cloth and steam for 1-1.5 hours, checking occasionally for doneness.
5. Serve with extra salsa or sour cream.

Pozole

Ingredients

- 2 lbs pork shoulder or chicken (cut into chunks)
- 1 onion, chopped
- 4 cloves garlic, minced
- 2 tbsp chili powder
- 2 tbsp oregano
- 6 cups chicken broth
- 2 cups hominy (canned or dried)
- 1/2 tsp cumin
- Salt to taste
- Toppings: Radishes, cilantro, onion, lime wedges, shredded cabbage, tostadas

Instructions

1. In a large pot, cook the pork or chicken with onion and garlic over medium heat for 5 minutes.
2. Add the chili powder, oregano, cumin, and salt, and stir for 1 minute.
3. Pour in the chicken broth and bring to a boil. Reduce heat to low and simmer for 1 hour, until the meat is tender.
4. Add the hominy and cook for an additional 30 minutes.
5. Serve with toppings like radishes, lime, shredded cabbage, and cilantro. Enjoy with tostadas.

Sopes

Ingredients

- 2 cups masa harina
- 1/2 cup warm water
- 1/4 tsp salt
- Vegetable oil for frying
- Toppings: Refried beans, shredded lettuce, cheese, sour cream, salsa

Instructions

1. In a bowl, mix masa harina, warm water, and salt until a dough forms.
2. Divide the dough into small balls and flatten them into thick disks.
3. Heat oil in a frying pan over medium heat and cook the sopes for about 2 minutes per side, until lightly browned.
4. Once fried, use your fingers to pinch the edges, creating a small "lip" around the edge of the sope.
5. Top with refried beans, lettuce, cheese, sour cream, and salsa. Serve immediately.

Mole Poblano

Ingredients

- 2 dried ancho chilies
- 2 dried pasilla chilies
- 2 dried mulato chilies
- 1/4 cup sesame seeds
- 1/4 cup almonds
- 1/4 cup pumpkin seeds
- 1 small onion, chopped
- 2 cloves garlic, minced
- 1/4 cup tomato paste
- 1/2 tsp cinnamon
- 1/2 tsp cumin
- 1/4 tsp cloves
- 1/4 tsp allspice
- 2 cups chicken broth
- 2 oz chocolate (unsweetened or semi-sweet)
- 2 tbsp vegetable oil
- Salt to taste

- Chicken, pork, or turkey for serving

Instructions

1. Toast the dried chilies in a hot, dry skillet for about 2 minutes until they become fragrant, then remove stems and seeds.

2. In a blender, combine the chilies, sesame seeds, almonds, pumpkin seeds, onion, garlic, tomato paste, and spices. Blend until smooth, adding chicken broth as needed to make a paste.

3. In a pan, heat the oil and cook the mole paste for 10 minutes, stirring frequently.

4. Add more chicken broth to thin the sauce if necessary, then simmer for an additional 15-20 minutes.

5. Stir in the chocolate and cook until melted and incorporated.

6. Serve over your choice of meat (chicken, pork, turkey), garnished with sesame seeds.

Quesadillas de Flor de Calabaza (Squash Blossom Quesadillas)

Ingredients

- 12-15 squash blossoms, cleaned and chopped
- 2 cups Oaxaca cheese (or Monterey Jack), shredded
- 1 small onion, finely chopped
- 1 tbsp vegetable oil
- 8 small corn tortillas
- Salt to taste

Instructions

1. In a skillet, heat the oil over medium heat. Add the onion and cook until soft, about 5 minutes.
2. Add the squash blossoms and cook for 2-3 minutes until tender. Season with salt.
3. Heat tortillas on a dry skillet until warm and pliable.
4. On one half of each tortilla, place a portion of the squash blossom mixture and top with cheese. Fold the tortilla in half.
5. Cook each quesadilla in the skillet for 2-3 minutes per side until golden brown and the cheese is melted.
6. Serve hot with salsa or crema.

Guacamole with Roasted Garlic

Ingredients:

- 3 ripe avocados, peeled, pitted, and mashed
- 4 cloves garlic, roasted (see instructions below)
- 1 small onion, finely chopped
- 1 medium tomato, chopped
- 1 lime, juiced
- 1-2 tbsp cilantro, chopped
- Salt and pepper to taste

Instructions:

1. To roast the garlic: Preheat the oven to 400°F (200°C). Wrap the garlic cloves in foil and roast for 20-25 minutes, until soft and fragrant. Once cooled, squeeze the roasted garlic out of the skins.
2. In a bowl, mash the avocados to your desired consistency.
3. Add the roasted garlic, chopped onion, tomato, lime juice, and cilantro to the mashed avocados.
4. Mix everything together, then season with salt and pepper to taste.
5. Serve immediately with tortilla chips or as a topping for your favorite Mexican dishes.

Chilaquiles

Ingredients:

- 10-12 corn tortillas, cut into triangles
- 1 cup red or green salsa
- 1 tbsp vegetable oil
- 1/2 cup onion, chopped
- 2 cups cooked chicken or pulled pork (optional)
- 2 eggs (fried or scrambled)
- 1/2 cup shredded cheese (queso fresco or cotija)
- 1/4 cup cilantro, chopped
- Sour cream for garnish (optional)
- Avocado slices for garnish (optional)
- Salt to taste

Instructions:

1. Heat the vegetable oil in a large skillet over medium heat. Fry the tortilla triangles until crispy and golden brown. Remove and drain on paper towels.
2. In the same skillet, sauté the chopped onion until translucent.
3. Add the salsa and cook for 2-3 minutes, allowing it to heat up.
4. Add the fried tortilla chips to the skillet and stir until coated with salsa. Cook for an additional 2-3 minutes until the chips soften slightly but still maintain some crunch.

5. Top with cooked chicken or pork (if desired), fried or scrambled eggs, cheese, cilantro, and optional garnishes like sour cream and avocado.

6. Serve immediately.

Carne Asada Burritos

Ingredients:

- 1 1/2 lbs flank steak or skirt steak
- 2 tbsp vegetable oil
- 2 cloves garlic, minced
- 1 lime, juiced
- 1 tbsp chili powder
- 1 tsp cumin
- 1 tsp paprika
- 1/2 tsp cayenne pepper (optional for spice)
- Salt and pepper to taste
- 4 large flour tortillas
- 1 cup cooked rice
- 1 cup black beans, drained and rinsed
- 1/2 cup salsa
- 1/2 cup guacamole
- 1/2 cup sour cream
- Fresh cilantro for garnish

Instructions:

1. Marinate the steak: In a bowl, combine the vegetable oil, garlic, lime juice, chili powder, cumin, paprika, cayenne (if using), salt, and pepper. Coat the steak in the marinade and refrigerate for at least 30 minutes (or up to 2 hours).

2. Grill the steak on medium-high heat for 4-5 minutes per side, depending on your desired level of doneness. Let it rest for a few minutes before slicing against the grain.

3. To assemble the burritos, warm the tortillas in a pan or microwave.

4. On each tortilla, layer a scoop of rice, black beans, grilled carne asada slices, salsa, guacamole, and sour cream.

5. Fold the sides of the tortilla in and roll it up tightly. Garnish with fresh cilantro.

6. Serve immediately.

Sopa de Lima

Ingredients:

- 1 lb chicken breast, boneless and skinless
- 1 tbsp olive oil
- 1 onion, chopped
- 2 cloves garlic, minced
- 1 large tomato, chopped
- 6 cups chicken broth
- 2 limes, juiced
- 1/2 tsp cumin
- 1/2 tsp oregano
- 1 bay leaf
- 1 medium zucchini, chopped
- 1 cup tortilla chips
- 1/2 cup fresh cilantro, chopped
- Salt and pepper to taste
- Lime wedges for garnish

Instructions:

1. In a large pot, heat olive oil over medium heat. Add the chicken breast and cook until browned on both sides. Remove and set aside to cool.

2. In the same pot, sauté the onion and garlic until soft and fragrant.

3. Add the tomato, chicken broth, lime juice, cumin, oregano, and bay leaf. Bring to a boil, then reduce heat and simmer for 10 minutes.

4. Shred the cooked chicken and return it to the pot. Add the chopped zucchini and cook for an additional 5 minutes.

5. Add tortilla chips and stir to combine. Simmer for another 2-3 minutes until the chips soften.

6. Remove the bay leaf and season with salt and pepper to taste.

7. Serve hot, garnished with cilantro and lime wedges.

Ceviche

Ingredients:

- 1 lb fresh white fish (such as tilapia or snapper), cut into small cubes
- 1/2 cup lime juice (from about 4 limes)
- 1/2 cup lemon juice (from about 2 lemons)
- 1/2 red onion, finely chopped
- 1 medium tomato, chopped
- 1/2 cucumber, peeled and chopped
- 1/4 cup cilantro, chopped
- 1 jalapeño, finely chopped (optional)
- Salt and pepper to taste

Instructions:

1. Place the fish cubes in a glass or ceramic bowl and cover with lime and lemon juice. Mix well and refrigerate for about 2-3 hours, until the fish becomes opaque.
2. Add the chopped onion, tomato, cucumber, cilantro, and jalapeño (if using) to the fish mixture.
3. Stir to combine, then season with salt and pepper to taste.
4. Serve chilled, accompanied by tortilla chips or on tostadas.

Baja Fish Tacos (with a twist)

Ingredients:

- 1 lb white fish fillets (such as cod or tilapia)
- 1/2 cup flour
- 1/2 cup cornmeal
- 1 tsp paprika
- 1 tsp cumin
- 1/2 tsp cayenne pepper
- Salt and pepper to taste
- 1 cup beer (or sparkling water for a non-alcoholic version)
- Vegetable oil for frying
- 8 small corn tortillas
- 1 cup cabbage, shredded
- 1/2 cup cilantro, chopped
- 1/4 cup lime juice
- 1/2 cup sour cream
- 1 tbsp chipotle sauce (or your favorite hot sauce)

Instructions:

1. Mix the flour, cornmeal, paprika, cumin, cayenne, salt, and pepper in a shallow dish.

2. Add beer (or sparkling water) and mix until a smooth batter forms.

3. Heat vegetable oil in a pan over medium-high heat.

4. Dip each fish fillet into the batter and fry until golden brown, about 2-3 minutes per side.

5. Warm the tortillas in a dry skillet or on a grill.

6. To assemble, place a few pieces of fried fish on each tortilla. Top with shredded cabbage, cilantro, and a drizzle of sour cream mixed with chipotle sauce.

7. Serve with lime wedges on the side.

Mexican Street Corn (Elote)

Ingredients:

- 4 ears of corn, husked
- 1/2 cup mayonnaise
- 1/2 cup cotija cheese, crumbled
- 1 tbsp chili powder
- 1 tbsp lime juice
- Salt to taste
- 1/4 cup cilantro, chopped (optional)

Instructions:

1. Grill the corn on medium-high heat for 10-12 minutes, turning occasionally until charred and tender.
2. In a small bowl, mix mayonnaise, chili powder, lime juice, and salt.
3. Once the corn is done, brush each ear with the mayo mixture.
4. Sprinkle with crumbled cotija cheese and cilantro.
5. Serve immediately with additional lime wedges.

Fajitas

Ingredients:

- 1 lb chicken breast, flank steak, or shrimp (your choice of protein)
- 2 tbsp vegetable oil
- 1 onion, sliced
- 1 bell pepper, sliced
- 1 zucchini, sliced
- 1 lime, juiced
- 1 tsp cumin
- 1 tsp chili powder
- 1/2 tsp paprika
- Salt and pepper to taste
- 8 small flour tortillas
- Toppings: Guacamole, sour cream, salsa, shredded cheese, cilantro

Instructions:

1. Heat oil in a large skillet over medium-high heat. Season the chicken, steak, or shrimp with cumin, chili powder, paprika, salt, and pepper.
2. Cook the protein until browned and cooked through. Remove from the skillet and set aside.
3. In the same skillet, sauté the onion, bell pepper, and zucchini until tender.

4. Slice the cooked protein and return it to the skillet with the veggies. Add lime juice and stir to combine.

5. Warm the tortillas in a pan or microwave.

6. Serve the fajita mixture in the tortillas, topping with your choice of guacamole, sour cream, salsa, cheese, and cilantro.

Empanadas de Pollo

Ingredients:

- 2 cups cooked chicken, shredded
- 1 small onion, finely chopped
- 2 cloves garlic, minced
- 1/2 cup tomato sauce
- 1/2 tsp cumin
- 1/2 tsp chili powder
- 1/4 tsp cinnamon (optional)
- 1/2 cup green olives, chopped
- 1/4 cup raisins
- 2 cups masa harina
- 1/2 cup warm water
- 1/4 cup vegetable oil (for frying)
- Salt and pepper to taste

Instructions:

1. In a skillet, heat some oil and sauté the onion and garlic until soft.
2. Add the shredded chicken, tomato sauce, cumin, chili powder, cinnamon, and salt and pepper. Cook for 5-7 minutes, allowing the flavors to combine. Stir in the chopped olives and raisins. Remove from heat and let it cool.

3. In a separate bowl, combine masa harina with warm water and a pinch of salt. Mix until a smooth dough forms. Let it rest for 10 minutes.

4. Divide the dough into small balls and roll each ball into a circle (about 4 inches in diameter).

5. Place a spoonful of the chicken filling in the center of each dough circle.

6. Fold the dough over to form a half-moon shape and press the edges with a fork to seal.

7. Heat oil in a pan and fry the empanadas for 2-3 minutes per side, until golden and crispy.

8. Serve with salsa or crema.

Rajas con Crema

Ingredients:

- 2 poblano peppers, roasted, peeled, and sliced
- 1 medium onion, sliced
- 1 cup heavy cream
- 1/2 cup shredded cheese (Mexican blend or Oaxaca cheese)
- 1 tbsp vegetable oil
- 1/2 tsp cumin
- Salt and pepper to taste

Instructions:

1. Heat oil in a large skillet over medium heat. Add the sliced onion and sauté until soft and golden.
2. Add the roasted poblano peppers to the skillet and cook for another 2-3 minutes.
3. Pour in the heavy cream and stir to combine. Cook for 5-7 minutes, allowing the cream to thicken slightly.
4. Add the shredded cheese and stir until melted and creamy. Season with cumin, salt, and pepper.
5. Serve as a side dish or as a topping for tacos or grilled meats.

Arroz con Pollo

Ingredients:

- 1 lb chicken thighs, bone-in and skin-on
- 2 tbsp vegetable oil
- 1 onion, chopped
- 2 cloves garlic, minced
- 1 bell pepper, chopped
- 1 cup long-grain rice
- 2 cups chicken broth
- 1 can (14 oz) diced tomatoes
- 1/2 cup frozen peas
- 1/4 tsp saffron or turmeric
- Salt and pepper to taste
- 1/2 cup cilantro, chopped (for garnish)

Instructions:

1. In a large skillet, heat the vegetable oil over medium-high heat. Season the chicken thighs with salt and pepper, then brown the chicken on both sides. Remove and set aside.
2. In the same skillet, sauté the onion, garlic, and bell pepper until soft.
3. Add the rice and stir to coat with the oil and vegetables. Cook for 2 minutes.

4. Pour in the chicken broth, diced tomatoes, and saffron (or turmeric). Stir and bring to a boil.

5. Return the chicken thighs to the skillet, skin-side up. Cover and simmer for 25-30 minutes, until the rice is cooked and the chicken is tender.

6. Add the frozen peas during the last 5 minutes of cooking.

7. Garnish with chopped cilantro before serving.

Pibil Tacos

Ingredients:

- 2 lbs pork shoulder, cut into chunks
- 3 cloves garlic, minced
- 1/4 cup achiote paste
- 1/4 cup orange juice
- 2 tbsp lime juice
- 1 tbsp cumin
- 1 tbsp oregano
- 1/4 tsp cinnamon
- Salt and pepper to taste
- 1 onion, thinly sliced
- 2 tbsp vinegar
- 8 small corn tortillas
- Cilantro and salsa for garnish

Instructions:

1. In a bowl, mix the minced garlic, achiote paste, orange juice, lime juice, cumin, oregano, cinnamon, salt, and pepper.
2. Coat the pork chunks with the marinade and refrigerate for at least 2 hours, preferably overnight.

3. Preheat the oven to 325°F (160°C). Place the marinated pork in a baking dish and cover tightly with foil.

4. Bake for 2-3 hours, until the pork is tender and easily shreds.

5. While the pork cooks, pickle the onion by combining it with vinegar, salt, and water. Let it sit for at least 30 minutes.

6. Shred the cooked pork with a fork and assemble the tacos by placing the pork on tortillas and topping with pickled onions, cilantro, and salsa.

7. Serve hot and enjoy!

Tostadas de Tinga

Ingredients:

- 2 cups shredded cooked chicken
- 1 can (14 oz) diced tomatoes
- 1 small onion, chopped
- 2 cloves garlic, minced
- 2 chipotle peppers in adobo sauce, chopped
- 1 tsp cumin
- 1 tsp oregano
- 1/2 cup chicken broth
- 8 tostada shells
- Refried beans (optional)
- Fresh cilantro, chopped
- Sour cream for garnish
- Avocado slices for garnish

Instructions:

1. In a skillet, heat a bit of oil and sauté the onion and garlic until soft.
2. Add the diced tomatoes, chipotle peppers, cumin, oregano, and chicken broth. Simmer for 10 minutes.

3. Stir in the shredded chicken and cook for another 5 minutes, until the chicken is heated through and coated in the sauce.

4. Spread a thin layer of refried beans on each tostada shell (optional).

5. Top with the chicken mixture, then garnish with cilantro, avocado slices, and sour cream.

6. Serve immediately.

Mexi-Pasta Salad

Ingredients:

- 1 lb elbow macaroni or penne pasta, cooked and drained
- 1 cup cherry tomatoes, halved
- 1/2 cup red onion, chopped
- 1/2 cup corn kernels (fresh or frozen)
- 1/2 cup black beans, drained and rinsed
- 1/2 cup cilantro, chopped
- 1 cup shredded cheddar cheese
- 1/2 cup sour cream
- 1/4 cup mayonnaise
- 1 tbsp lime juice
- 1 tsp chili powder
- Salt and pepper to taste

Instructions:

1. In a large bowl, combine the cooked pasta, tomatoes, red onion, corn, black beans, cilantro, and cheddar cheese.
2. In a separate bowl, whisk together the sour cream, mayonnaise, lime juice, chili powder, salt, and pepper.
3. Pour the dressing over the pasta salad and mix to combine.

4. Chill in the refrigerator for 30 minutes before serving.

Prawn Aguachile

Ingredients:

- 1 lb large shrimp, peeled and deveined
- 1/4 cup lime juice
- 1/4 cup orange juice
- 1/2 tsp salt
- 1 serrano chili, chopped
- 1/4 cup cucumber, thinly sliced
- 1/4 red onion, thinly sliced
- 1/4 cup cilantro, chopped

Instructions:

1. Slice the shrimp in half lengthwise and place them in a glass dish.
2. In a blender, combine lime juice, orange juice, salt, serrano chili, and cilantro. Blend until smooth.
3. Pour the sauce over the shrimp and refrigerate for at least 30 minutes to allow the shrimp to "cook" in the citrus juices.
4. Add the sliced cucumber and red onion and stir gently.
5. Garnish with additional cilantro and serve chilled.

Churros

Ingredients:

- 1 cup water
- 1/2 cup unsalted butter
- 1 tbsp sugar
- 1/4 tsp salt
- 1 cup all-purpose flour
- 2 large eggs
- Vegetable oil for frying
- 1/2 cup sugar
- 1 tsp ground cinnamon

Instructions:

1. In a saucepan, bring water, butter, sugar, and salt to a boil over medium heat.
2. Add the flour and stir vigorously until the dough pulls away from the sides of the pan.
3. Remove from heat and allow to cool slightly. Add the eggs one at a time, stirring until smooth after each addition.
4. Heat oil in a frying pan over medium-high heat.
5. Spoon the dough into a pastry bag fitted with a star tip.
6. Pipe 4-6 inch lengths of dough into the hot oil, frying until golden and crispy. Remove and drain on paper towels.

7. In a small bowl, combine the sugar and cinnamon. Roll the hot churros in the mixture and serve warm.

Chile con Carne

Ingredients:

- 1 lb ground beef
- 1 onion, chopped
- 2 cloves garlic, minced
- 1 can (14 oz) diced tomatoes
- 2 tbsp chili powder
- 1 tsp cumin
- 1 tsp paprika
- 1/2 tsp oregano
- 1/2 tsp cayenne pepper (optional)
- 1 cup beef broth
- Salt and pepper to taste
- 1/2 cup kidney beans or pinto beans (optional)
- 1/2 cup shredded cheddar cheese (optional)
- Sour cream for garnish (optional)

Instructions:

1. In a large skillet, brown the ground beef over medium heat, breaking it up into small pieces as it cooks. Drain excess fat.
2. Add the chopped onion and garlic, and sauté until the onion is soft.

3. Stir in the diced tomatoes, chili powder, cumin, paprika, oregano, cayenne, and beef broth. Bring to a simmer.

4. Cook for 20-30 minutes, allowing the flavors to meld and the sauce to thicken.

5. If using beans, stir them in during the last 10 minutes of cooking.

6. Season with salt and pepper to taste.

7. Serve with shredded cheese and a dollop of sour cream, if desired.

Huevos Rancheros

Ingredients:

- 4 large eggs
- 4 corn tortillas
- 1 cup salsa (homemade or store-bought)
- 1/2 cup refried beans
- 1/4 cup shredded cheese (cheddar, Oaxaca, or cotija)
- 1/4 cup fresh cilantro, chopped
- 1/4 cup sour cream (optional)
- 1 tbsp vegetable oil
- Salt and pepper to taste

Instructions:

1. Heat the tortillas in a dry skillet until warm and slightly crispy. Set aside.
2. In a large skillet, heat oil over medium heat. Crack the eggs into the skillet, cooking until the whites are set but the yolks are still runny (or cook to your preferred level).
3. Warm the salsa in a small saucepan over low heat.
4. To assemble, place each tortilla on a plate. Spread a thin layer of refried beans on each tortilla.
5. Place a cooked egg on top of the beans. Spoon warm salsa over the egg, then sprinkle with shredded cheese and cilantro.

6. Serve with a dollop of sour cream, if desired.

Mexican Rice

Ingredients:

- 1 cup long-grain white rice
- 2 tbsp vegetable oil
- 1/2 onion, chopped
- 2 cloves garlic, minced
- 1 can (14 oz) diced tomatoes
- 2 cups chicken broth
- 1/2 tsp cumin
- 1/2 tsp paprika
- Salt to taste
- Fresh cilantro for garnish (optional)

Instructions:

1. Rinse the rice under cold water until the water runs clear.
2. In a large skillet, heat the oil over medium heat. Add the rice and cook, stirring constantly, until it turns golden brown.
3. Add the chopped onion and garlic, cooking for another 2-3 minutes until softened.
4. Stir in the diced tomatoes (with juices), chicken broth, cumin, paprika, and salt. Bring to a boil.

5. Reduce heat to low, cover, and cook for 20-25 minutes, or until the rice is tender and the liquid has been absorbed.

6. Fluff the rice with a fork and garnish with fresh cilantro, if desired.

Poblano Soup

Ingredients:

- 4 poblano peppers, roasted, peeled, and chopped
- 1 medium onion, chopped
- 2 cloves garlic, minced
- 4 cups chicken broth
- 1 cup heavy cream
- 1 tbsp vegetable oil
- 1/2 tsp cumin
- Salt and pepper to taste
- 1/2 cup shredded cheese (optional)
- Fresh cilantro for garnish (optional)

Instructions:

1. In a large pot, heat the oil over medium heat. Add the chopped onion and garlic, sautéing until soft.
2. Add the roasted poblano peppers and cumin, and cook for another 2 minutes.
3. Pour in the chicken broth and bring the soup to a simmer. Cook for 10-15 minutes to blend the flavors.
4. Use an immersion blender to blend the soup until smooth (or transfer to a blender in batches).

5. Stir in the heavy cream and cook for an additional 5 minutes. Season with salt and pepper to taste.

6. Serve garnished with shredded cheese and cilantro, if desired.

Capirotada (Mexican Bread Pudding)

Ingredients:

- 4 cups cubed stale bolillo or French bread
- 1 1/2 cups brown sugar
- 2 cups water
- 1 cinnamon stick
- 3 cloves
- 1/2 cup raisins
- 1/2 cup chopped pecans or walnuts
- 1/2 cup shredded coconut (optional)
- 1/2 tsp vanilla extract
- 2 tbsp butter, melted
- 2 large eggs, beaten

Instructions:

1. Preheat the oven to 350°F (175°C). Grease a 9x13-inch baking dish.
2. In a saucepan, combine the water, brown sugar, cinnamon stick, and cloves. Bring to a boil and simmer for 5 minutes. Remove from heat and stir in the vanilla extract.
3. In the prepared baking dish, layer the bread cubes, raisins, nuts, and coconut.
4. Pour the sugar syrup over the bread, ensuring it soaks the bread evenly. Let it sit for 10 minutes.

5. Whisk the beaten eggs with melted butter and pour it over the soaked bread mixture.

6. Bake for 35-40 minutes, or until the pudding is golden brown and set.

7. Serve warm, optionally with a drizzle of cream or vanilla sauce.

Mexican Cornbread

Ingredients:

- 1 cup cornmeal
- 1 cup all-purpose flour
- 1/4 cup sugar
- 2 tbsp baking powder
- 1/2 tsp salt
- 1 cup milk
- 2 large eggs
- 1/4 cup melted butter
- 1/2 cup shredded cheddar cheese (optional)

Instructions:

1. Preheat the oven to 400°F (200°C). Grease a 9-inch square baking dish.
2. In a large bowl, combine the cornmeal, flour, sugar, baking powder, and salt.
3. In a separate bowl, whisk together the milk, eggs, and melted butter.
4. Pour the wet ingredients into the dry ingredients and stir until just combined. If using cheese, fold it in at this point.
5. Pour the batter into the prepared baking dish and bake for 20-25 minutes, or until golden and a toothpick inserted in the center comes out clean.
6. Serve warm with butter.

Chorizo con Papas

Ingredients:

- 1 lb chorizo sausage, casing removed
- 2 medium potatoes, peeled and diced
- 1 onion, chopped
- 1/2 tsp cumin
- Salt and pepper to taste
- Fresh cilantro for garnish (optional)

Instructions:

1. In a large skillet, cook the chorizo over medium heat until browned, breaking it up into small pieces as it cooks.
2. Remove the chorizo from the skillet and set aside. In the same skillet, add the diced potatoes and cook until golden and tender, about 10 minutes.
3. Add the chopped onion and cumin to the skillet, cooking until the onion is soft.
4. Return the chorizo to the skillet, mixing it with the potatoes. Cook for an additional 5 minutes.
5. Season with salt and pepper, and garnish with fresh cilantro, if desired.

Molletes

Ingredients:

- 4 bolillo rolls, halved lengthwise
- 1 cup refried beans
- 1 cup shredded cheese (Oaxaca, mozzarella, or cheddar)
- 1/4 cup pico de gallo or salsa
- 1/2 tsp cumin (optional)
- Butter for toasting

Instructions:

1. Preheat the broiler in your oven.
2. Spread a thin layer of butter on the cut sides of the bolillo rolls. Toast them under the broiler for 2-3 minutes, until golden and crispy.
3. Spread a layer of refried beans on each toasted roll half.
4. Sprinkle with shredded cheese and place the rolls under the broiler again until the cheese melts and is bubbly, about 2-3 minutes.
5. Top with pico de gallo or salsa and sprinkle with cumin, if desired. Serve immediately.

Panuchos

Ingredients:

- 8 small corn tortillas
- 1/2 cup refried black beans
- 1 lb cooked chicken, shredded
- 1/2 cup lettuce, shredded
- 1/2 cup tomato, chopped
- 1/2 avocado, sliced
- 1/4 cup pickled red onions
- Salsa for garnish

Instructions:

1. Heat the tortillas in a skillet until lightly toasted.
2. Spread a thin layer of refried black beans on each tortilla.
3. Top with shredded chicken, shredded lettuce, chopped tomato, avocado slices, and pickled red onions.
4. Drizzle with salsa and serve immediately.

Tacos de Carnitas

Ingredients:

- 2 lbs pork shoulder, cut into chunks
- 1 onion, quartered
- 4 cloves garlic, smashed
- 2 oranges, juiced
- 1 tsp cumin
- 1 tsp oregano
- 2 bay leaves
- Salt and pepper to taste
- Corn tortillas
- Toppings: chopped cilantro, diced onions, salsa, lime wedges

Instructions:

1. In a large pot, combine the pork, onion, garlic, orange juice, cumin, oregano, and bay leaves. Add enough water to cover the pork.
2. Bring to a boil, then reduce the heat and simmer for 2-3 hours, or until the pork is tender and easily shreds.
3. Remove the pork from the pot and shred it with two forks.
4. Heat a skillet over medium-high heat and cook the shredded pork in batches until crispy and browned on the edges.

5. Serve the carnitas in warm corn tortillas, topped with cilantro, onions, salsa, and lime wedges.

Picadillo

Ingredients:

- 1 lb ground beef
- 1 onion, chopped
- 2 cloves garlic, minced
- 1/2 cup raisins
- 1/2 cup diced potatoes, peeled and cubed
- 1/2 cup carrots, diced
- 1/4 cup chopped green olives
- 1/4 cup chopped almonds (optional)
- 1 can (14 oz) diced tomatoes
- 1/2 cup beef broth
- 1 tsp cumin
- 1 tsp cinnamon
- Salt and pepper to taste
- Fresh cilantro for garnish

Instructions:

1. In a large skillet, brown the ground beef over medium heat, breaking it up into small pieces. Drain excess fat.
2. Add the chopped onion and garlic, and sauté until the onion is soft.

3. Stir in the raisins, potatoes, carrots, olives, and almonds (if using), and cook for 5-7 minutes.

4. Add the diced tomatoes, beef broth, cumin, and cinnamon. Bring to a simmer.

5. Cover and cook for 20-25 minutes until the potatoes and carrots are tender.

6. Season with salt and pepper to taste, and garnish with fresh cilantro.

7. Serve with rice or tortillas.

Salsa Verde

Ingredients:

- 10-12 tomatillos, husked and rinsed
- 1-2 jalapeños (or to taste)
- 1/2 onion, chopped
- 1/2 cup fresh cilantro
- 2 cloves garlic
- Salt to taste
- 1 cup water or more for desired consistency

Instructions:

1. In a pot, bring water to a boil. Add the tomatillos and jalapeños, cooking for 5-7 minutes, or until the tomatillos are soft and their skin begins to split.
2. Drain and let them cool slightly.
3. Blend the tomatillos, jalapeños, onion, cilantro, garlic, and salt in a blender or food processor until smooth. Add water gradually to achieve the desired consistency.
4. Taste and adjust seasoning as needed.
5. Serve with tacos, grilled meats, or chips.

Tarta de Tres Leches (Three Milk Cake)

Ingredients:

For the cake:

- 1 1/2 cups all-purpose flour
- 1 1/2 tsp baking powder
- 1/4 tsp salt
- 5 large eggs
- 1 cup sugar
- 1/2 cup milk
- 1 tsp vanilla extract

For the tres leches mixture:

- 1 can (12 oz) evaporated milk
- 1 can (14 oz) sweetened condensed milk
- 1 cup heavy cream

For the topping:

- 1 cup heavy cream
- 2 tbsp powdered sugar
- 1 tsp vanilla extract

Instructions:

1. Preheat the oven to 350°F (175°C). Grease and flour a 9x13-inch baking dish.

2. In a bowl, whisk together the flour, baking powder, and salt.

3. In a separate bowl, beat the eggs with sugar until pale and fluffy, about 5 minutes.

4. Mix in the milk and vanilla extract. Gradually add the dry ingredients, mixing until smooth.

5. Pour the batter into the prepared baking dish and bake for 20-25 minutes, or until a toothpick comes out clean.

6. Once the cake is done, let it cool slightly. While it cools, mix together the evaporated milk, condensed milk, and heavy cream.

7. Once the cake has cooled a bit, poke holes in it with a fork and slowly pour the milk mixture over the cake, allowing it to soak in.

8. Whip the heavy cream with powdered sugar and vanilla extract until stiff peaks form, then spread over the cake.

9. Refrigerate for at least 4 hours before serving.

Caldo de Res (Beef Soup)

Ingredients:

- 2 lbs beef shank or stew meat
- 1 onion, quartered
- 2 cloves garlic, minced
- 1 carrot, peeled and chopped
- 1 celery stalk, chopped
- 2 medium potatoes, peeled and diced
- 2 corn on the cob, cut into thirds
- 1 zucchini, chopped
- 1/2 head cabbage, chopped
- 1 cup cilantro, chopped
- 2-3 chiles guajillo, seeds removed
- 8 cups water or beef broth
- Salt and pepper to taste
- Lime wedges for garnish

Instructions:

1. In a large pot, combine the beef, onion, garlic, and water (or beef broth). Bring to a boil, then lower the heat and simmer for 1-1.5 hours, until the beef is tender.
2. Remove the beef and shred it. Discard any bones and fat.

3. Add the carrots, celery, potatoes, and corn to the pot. Cook for another 10-15 minutes, until the vegetables are tender.

4. Stir in the zucchini, cabbage, cilantro, and guajillo chiles. Simmer for an additional 10 minutes.

5. Season with salt and pepper to taste.

6. Serve hot, garnished with lime wedges and additional cilantro.

Cochinita Pibil

Ingredients:

- 2 lbs pork shoulder, cut into chunks
- 3 tbsp achiote paste
- 1/2 cup orange juice
- 1/4 cup white vinegar
- 1 tsp cumin
- 1 tsp oregano
- 2 cloves garlic, minced
- 1 onion, thinly sliced
- Banana leaves or foil for wrapping
- Salt and pepper to taste
- Pickled red onions for garnish

Instructions:

1. In a blender, combine the achiote paste, orange juice, vinegar, cumin, oregano, garlic, and a pinch of salt. Blend until smooth.
2. Place the pork chunks in a large bowl and pour the marinade over them. Mix to coat evenly. Cover and refrigerate for at least 4 hours or overnight.
3. Preheat the oven to 325°F (165°C).
4. Line a baking dish with banana leaves or foil. Place the marinated pork in the dish, cover with more banana leaves (or foil), and bake for 2-3 hours until the

pork is tender.

5. Shred the pork with two forks and season with salt and pepper.

6. Serve with pickled red onions and tortillas.

Birria

Ingredients:

- 2 lbs beef (chuck or short ribs), cut into chunks
- 2 dried guajillo chiles
- 2 dried ancho chiles
- 2 dried pasilla chiles
- 1 onion, quartered
- 4 cloves garlic
- 1 tsp cumin
- 1 tsp oregano
- 1 cinnamon stick
- 2 bay leaves
- 4 cups beef broth
- 1 tbsp vinegar
- Salt to taste
- Corn tortillas for serving

Instructions:

1. Toast the chiles lightly in a dry pan for a few seconds, then soak them in hot water for 10-15 minutes until softened.

2. Blend the soaked chiles with the onion, garlic, cumin, oregano, cinnamon, and vinegar until smooth.

3. In a large pot, combine the beef, bay leaves, and beef broth. Bring to a boil, then lower the heat and simmer for 2-3 hours, until the beef is tender.

4. Add the blended chile mixture to the pot and continue cooking for another 30 minutes.

5. Shred the beef with two forks and adjust seasoning with salt.

6. Serve with warm tortillas, dipping the tortillas in the broth, and garnish with chopped onions, cilantro, and lime.

Relleno de Pollo (Chicken Stuffed with Vegetables)

Ingredients:

- 4 boneless, skinless chicken breasts
- 1 cup spinach, chopped
- 1/2 cup mushrooms, chopped
- 1/2 cup bell peppers, chopped
- 1/2 cup cream cheese
- 1/4 cup shredded cheese (cheddar or mozzarella)
- 2 cloves garlic, minced
- Salt and pepper to taste
- Olive oil for searing

Instructions:

1. Preheat the oven to 375°F (190°C).
2. In a skillet, sauté the spinach, mushrooms, bell peppers, and garlic in olive oil until softened.
3. In a bowl, mix the sautéed vegetables with cream cheese and shredded cheese. Season with salt and pepper.
4. Slice a pocket into the chicken breasts and stuff them with the vegetable mixture.
5. Heat olive oil in an oven-safe skillet over medium-high heat. Sear the stuffed chicken breasts on both sides until golden brown.

6. Transfer the skillet to the oven and bake for 20-25 minutes, until the chicken is fully cooked.

7. Serve with a side of rice or roasted vegetables.

Papas con Chorizo

Ingredients:

- 2 medium potatoes, peeled and diced
- 1/2 lb chorizo sausage
- 1/2 onion, chopped
- 1/4 cup fresh cilantro, chopped
- Salt to taste

Instructions:

1. Boil the diced potatoes in salted water for 10 minutes, or until tender. Drain and set aside.
2. In a skillet, cook the chorizo over medium heat until browned, breaking it up into small pieces.
3. Add the chopped onion and cook until softened.
4. Stir in the boiled potatoes and cook for another 5-7 minutes until crispy.
5. Garnish with chopped cilantro and serve with warm tortillas.

Mexican Hot Chocolate

Ingredients:

- 4 cups milk
- 1/2 cup dark chocolate, chopped
- 2 tbsp sugar
- 1 cinnamon stick
- 1/4 tsp vanilla extract
- A pinch of chili powder (optional)

Instructions:

1. In a saucepan, heat the milk over medium heat until hot but not boiling.
2. Add the dark chocolate, sugar, and cinnamon stick. Stir until the chocolate melts and the mixture is smooth.
3. Add the vanilla extract and a pinch of chili powder, if using. Stir to combine.
4. Pour the hot chocolate into mugs and serve warm.

Chilaquiles Rojos

Ingredients:

- 12 corn tortillas, cut into wedges
- 2 cups red salsa (store-bought or homemade)
- 1/2 cup chicken broth
- 2 tbsp vegetable oil
- 1/2 cup onion, chopped
- 2 cloves garlic, minced
- 1/2 cup crumbled queso fresco
- 1/4 cup sour cream
- Fresh cilantro, chopped
- 1-2 boiled eggs, sliced (optional)
- Salt to taste

Instructions:

1. Heat vegetable oil in a large skillet over medium heat. Fry the tortilla wedges until golden and crispy, then remove and drain on paper towels.
2. In the same skillet, sauté the onion and garlic until softened.
3. Add the red salsa and chicken broth, bringing the mixture to a simmer. Cook for 5-7 minutes until the sauce thickens slightly.
4. Add the fried tortilla wedges to the skillet, stirring gently to coat with the sauce.

5. Serve topped with crumbled queso fresco, sour cream, boiled eggs (optional), and chopped cilantro.

6. Season with salt to taste.

Tacos de Lengua (Beef Tongue Tacos)

Ingredients:

- 1 beef tongue (about 3 lbs)
- 1 onion, halved
- 2 garlic cloves
- 2 bay leaves
- 1 tbsp cumin
- 1 tbsp oregano
- 1/2 tsp black pepper
- 1/4 tsp cloves (optional)
- Salt to taste
- 12 small corn tortillas
- Salsa (optional)
- Fresh cilantro, chopped
- Lime wedges

Instructions:

1. Rinse the beef tongue and place it in a large pot. Cover with water and add onion, garlic, bay leaves, cumin, oregano, black pepper, and salt.

2. Bring the water to a boil, then lower the heat and simmer for 3-4 hours, until the tongue is tender and easily pierced with a fork.

3. Once cooked, remove the tongue and peel off the tough outer skin. Slice the tongue into small pieces.

4. Warm the tortillas and fill with the sliced tongue.

5. Top with fresh cilantro, salsa, and a squeeze of lime.

Pescado a la Veracruzana (Veracruz-Style Fish)

Ingredients:

- 4 fish fillets (red snapper or any firm white fish)
- 2 tbsp olive oil
- 1 onion, sliced
- 2 cloves garlic, minced
- 2 tomatoes, diced
- 1/2 cup green olives, pitted and chopped
- 1/4 cup capers
- 1/2 cup white wine
- 1/2 cup fish stock or water
- 1/4 tsp cumin
- 1/2 tsp dried oregano
- 1/4 tsp chili flakes (optional)
- Fresh cilantro, chopped
- Lime wedges
- Salt and pepper to taste

Instructions:

1. Heat olive oil in a skillet over medium heat. Season the fish fillets with salt and pepper.

2. Cook the fish fillets for 3-4 minutes per side, until golden and cooked through. Remove from the skillet and set aside.

3. In the same skillet, add onion and garlic, cooking until softened. Add tomatoes, olives, capers, white wine, fish stock, cumin, oregano, and chili flakes (if using).

4. Let the sauce simmer for 10-15 minutes until it thickens slightly.

5. Return the fish fillets to the skillet and simmer for another 5 minutes, allowing the flavors to meld together.

6. Serve with fresh cilantro, lime wedges, and additional sauce spooned over the fish.

Salsa Roja

Ingredients:

- 6-8 roma tomatoes
- 2 dried guajillo chiles
- 1-2 jalapeños (optional, for extra heat)
- 1/4 onion, chopped
- 2 cloves garlic
- 1/2 tsp cumin
- Salt to taste
- 1/2 cup water

Instructions:

1. Heat a dry skillet over medium heat. Toast the guajillo chiles until fragrant, about 2-3 minutes. Remove the stems and seeds.
2. Boil the tomatoes, guajillo chiles, jalapeños (optional), onion, and garlic in a pot for about 10 minutes, or until softened.
3. Blend the cooked ingredients with cumin and salt in a blender until smooth, adding water to reach the desired consistency.
4. Taste and adjust seasoning if necessary. Use as a topping for tacos, grilled meats, or chips.

Tostadas de Ceviche

Ingredients:

- 1 lb fresh fish fillets (tilapia, snapper, or sea bass), cut into small cubes
- 1 cup fresh lime juice
- 1/2 red onion, finely chopped
- 1 cucumber, peeled and diced
- 1 tomato, diced
- 1/2 cup chopped cilantro
- 1-2 serrano chilies, finely chopped (optional)
- Salt and pepper to taste
- 8-10 tostada shells
- Avocado slices (optional)

Instructions:

1. In a bowl, combine the cubed fish with lime juice. Stir well, ensuring the fish is fully coated. Cover and refrigerate for 3-4 hours, allowing the fish to "cook" in the lime juice.
2. Once the fish is opaque and firm, add the onion, cucumber, tomato, cilantro, serrano chilies (optional), and season with salt and pepper.
3. Spoon the ceviche mixture onto tostada shells and top with avocado slices.
4. Serve immediately.

Tamal de Elote (Sweet Corn Tamales)

Ingredients:

- 2 cups fresh corn kernels (or frozen, thawed)
- 1/2 cup masa harina
- 1/2 cup sugar
- 1/2 tsp baking powder
- 1/4 tsp salt
- 1/2 cup melted butter
- 1 cup milk
- 1 tsp vanilla extract
- 12-15 corn husks, soaked

Instructions:

1. In a blender, blend the corn kernels with milk until smooth. Set aside.
2. In a large mixing bowl, combine masa harina, sugar, baking powder, and salt.
3. Add the melted butter, vanilla, and corn mixture to the dry ingredients, stirring to combine.
4. Spread the masa mixture onto soaked corn husks and fold the sides in to form a pocket.
5. Steam the tamales in a large pot for about 1-1.5 hours, until the masa is cooked through and separates easily from the husk.
6. Serve with a dollop of crema or salsa.

Tacos al Pastor

Ingredients:

- 2 lbs pork shoulder, thinly sliced
- 1/4 cup achiote paste
- 1/2 cup pineapple juice
- 1/4 cup white vinegar
- 1 tsp cumin
- 1 tsp oregano
- 1/2 tsp chili powder
- Salt and pepper to taste
- 1/2 pineapple, sliced
- 12 small corn tortillas
- Chopped onion and cilantro for garnish
- Lime wedges

Instructions:

1. In a bowl, combine achiote paste, pineapple juice, vinegar, cumin, oregano, chili powder, salt, and pepper. Marinate the pork in this mixture for at least 4 hours or overnight.

2. Grill or cook the pork slices on a hot grill or skillet until cooked through and slightly caramelized.

3. Grill the pineapple slices until charred, then cut into small pieces.

4. Warm the tortillas and fill with the cooked pork, garnishing with grilled pineapple, chopped onion, cilantro, and lime wedges.

Arroz con Leche (Mexican Rice Pudding)

Ingredients:

- 1 cup white rice
- 4 cups whole milk
- 1/2 cup sugar
- 1/2 tsp cinnamon
- 1 tsp vanilla extract
- 1/4 cup raisins (optional)
- Ground cinnamon for garnish

Instructions:

1. In a pot, combine the rice and 2 cups of water. Bring to a boil, then reduce the heat and simmer for 10 minutes. Drain excess water.
2. Add the milk, sugar, cinnamon, vanilla, and raisins (optional) to the rice, and bring to a simmer.
3. Cook for about 20-25 minutes, stirring occasionally, until the rice is tender and the pudding thickens.
4. Serve warm or chilled, garnished with ground cinnamon.